DUNNS'
FIVE
LESSONS

ORIGINAL GOLF FUNDAMENTALS

Musselburgh, Scotland
Ronald Ross 1858

Ronald Ross 1858 · 50933 Cologne Germany

Publishing services by Lumphanan Press
www.lumphananpress.co.uk

ISBN: 978-3-00-059837-1

Cover design: Ronald Ross 1858
www.originalgolffundamentalsdunns5lessons.com

As Presented
"To H. H. Ramsay President U.S.G.A. 1932"

Part 1 – GEOMETRICS
Learn of the Five Mechanical Laws of the Golf Swing
– Fundamentals 1 to 5 – to become consistently
accurate. Deals with matters pertaining to accuracy of
swing only.

After a seven years' search, and practice, in seeking to cure a slice and wanting to play good golf, it has been determined that the Home of the Original Golf Fundamentals is Musselburgh, Scotland, and that the Original Golf Fundamentals Dunns' Five Lessons are, still, the essentials of golf! The evidence is now before you. Also see our web site and trust in Sir Henry Cotton at:

www.originalgolffundamentalsdunns5lessons.com

Contents

Introduction
Dunns' Five Lessons

This book is intended as a reminder of the principal points to study in the science of the game. The subject matter of this book is the text by which all instructors taught in the Seymour Dunn Golf School at Lake Placid, N.Y.

"To excel at the game, one should go about it correctly. Since many golfers achieve success with wide varieties of stance, grip, body pivot, etc., it stands to reason that while of very great importance, such matters are not fundamentals of the golf swing. They are merely matters of style and of method in applying the fundamentals. Fundamentals are basic principles of a theory and these principles should be regarded as inviolable by the student no matter what the expert players may do and get way with. It is to be regretted that many writers use the term "fundamental" loosely when discussing matters of style, individual mannerisms, or other important, but not fundamental, aspects of golf."

GOLF FUNDAMENTALS BY SEYMOUR DUNN 1922, STANDARDIZED GOLF INSTRUCTION SEYMOUR DUNN 1934

The Golf Swing

There are many styles of the golf swing: long, short, and medium, also upright, flat, and orthodox. Then again there are swings that are all shoulder action or all arm action or all wrist action. Some swings are a combination of shoulders and arms while others are hips and wrists, any of which may be good, but a combination of hips, shoulders, arms and wrists is more likely to give greatest distance.

There are certain fundamental principles of the swing which the good player must observe and these are set forth in the following pages under the title of Original Golf Fundamentals Dunns' Five Lessons.

PART 1

Learn of the Five Mechanical Laws
of the Golf Swing –
Fundamentals 1 to 5
– to become consistently accurate

MECHANICAL PRINCIPLES

By closely observing the following Mechanical principles you are certain to improve, and by analyzing your strokes according to these mechanical principles, you can find a clear and logical explanation for any and all your troubles.

To dispatch the ball correctly in a given direction, we must have the three following essentials:

1. Strike with the centre of the club face.

2. Club head must be travelling in the direction of play during the impact.

3. Club face must be at right angles to the direction of play.

To ensure these ends we should build up our swing on the following mechanical principles, and we should regard these mechanical principles as the mechanical laws of our swing.

Failure to accomplish Essential 1 is due to violation of one or more of these:

1. Maintain a steady swing centre.

2. Maintain a proper swing radius.

3. Swing club in a proper plane of obliquity.

4. Swing club parallel to intended direction of play.

5. Club face must be controlled so that it is square to the intended direction of play at the moment of impact.

These principles are all set forth in this series of lessons and each lesson should be mastered before proceeding to the next. By mastered, I mean not merely understood but practiced till physical application has become second nature – unconscious habit.

Epigraph
Sir Henry Cotton

"After over fifty years in the game, as a professional, championship winner and teacher, I feel I have earned the right to speak my mind on the game of golf, hoping that my words will reach at least some of the twenty million or so people throughout the world who enjoy, and sometimes suffer from, their involvement in this greatest of all sports."

"Sixty years ago I remember that outstanding instructor Seymour Dunn proclaiming that golf was 85 per cent hands and only 15 per cent body. Nothing in a lifetime's experience in golf has happened to make me think otherwise. How right he has been!"

"Many of the old champions stressed that 'when your legs go, you are through winning'; Sam Snead during his 1979 trip to Australia announced that he was almost through with competing in the 'big leagues' for his legs had gone, and of course strong legs are essential for control. Accept this as a fact, learn to use the hands properly, and like me you will enjoy a lifetime of pleasure-golf."

THANKS FOR THE GAME The Best of Golf with HENRY COTTON Sidgwick & Jackson London Henry Cotton Penina 1980.

Author's Genealogy

The articles contained herein are the result of the life study handed down by many generations.

PROFESSIONAL GOLFERS OF MUSSELBOROUGH, SCOTLAND

"Old" Willie Dunn, the famous Professional Golfer of Musselborough, Scotland, who played in the Great Golf Match of 1849, with his brother Jamie Dunn against Allen Robinson and Tom Morris for four hundred pounds sterling a side, was the father of the yet more famous Tom Dunn of North Berwick, Scotland, who from the time he was 20 years old till he died at the age of 52 was universally acknowledged the leading authority on golf.

I am the youngest son of Tom Dunn. I was born at North Berwick, Scotland, March 11th, in the year of 1882 and, as my forefathers did, I cut my first teeth on a golf club.

On my mother's side were the Gourlays of Musselborough, and my mother Isabella Gourlay, true to her family traditions, was the greatest woman golfer of her day. Her father, John Gourlay, was the famous leather and feather golf ball maker. He was also a golfer of great renown.

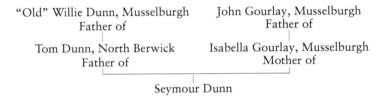

"Old" Willie Dunn, Musselburgh
Father of

John Gourlay, Musselburgh
Father of

Tom Dunn, North Berwick
Father of

Isabella Gourlay, Musselburgh
Mother of

Seymour Dunn

Dunn Gourlay Family Tree

Back farther still on my mother's side there was a Douglas Gourlay, who was appointed teacher of golf to James V of Scotland. All these family connections have been a great help in preparing me for the great object of my life, which is to get down to the very root of this great problem, "The Fundamentals of Golf".

I have not indulged in practicing my own play for the capture of championship honors but have devoted myself to studying the science of the game, and analyzing every detail connected with it. I chose the work of a teacher as the best field for study for there all manner of questions arise and have to be met with a perfectly clear, correct and understandable explanation.

In the twenty years that I have been teaching Golf, I must have given as many if not more golf lessons than any other teacher that ever lived, and I hope among you, my dear children, there will arise at least one, a wielder of the club able to uphold the name of Dunn.

*Musselborough was the original centre of golf, much older than St. Andrews.

SEYMOUR DUNN

Don't forget: Strong hands and wrists are most essential to the golfer. Be sure to develop your hands by regular exercise with a wrist machine

Part 1 – GEOMETRICS
Learn of the Five Mechanical
Laws of the Golf Swing

FUNDAMENTAL 1
A Steady Swing Centre

A steady centre is essential to a steady swing.

Centre of shoulders is centre of swing.

Proper body action will keep centre steady.

If player's head is steady, swing centre will be steady.

Warning – the best of intentions sometimes fail; therefore, do not be too sure of what you do. You may feel sure your head did not move, while it actually moved several inches.

This applies alike to all the following:

If the player's head is to be kept steady, the player's body must turn on a pivot. Since the human body has two pivotal points, i. e., the hip joints, and since it is impossible to pivot on two points at the same time, we must choose between them, as experience has taught us that it is no use attempting to pivot upon an imaginary pivotal centre between the two.

A close study of our greatest golfers reveals the fact that when they turn their bodies to the right they pivot upon the right hip, and, when they turn to the left they pivot upon the left hip. They shift from one hip to the other, yet they do this without moving their heads, by shifting the middle part of their body weight only.

To Shift the Pivotal Centre

To shift the pivotal centre, we must shift our centre of gravity. To pivot on the right hip we must shift the greater part of our body weight to the right foot, and shift it to the left foot to pivot on the left hip. All this body weight shifting movement is done with sidewise hip action.

At the address position of the golf swing, the player's weight is equally divided between the two feet. Then as the upswing starts and the player's body has to turn, the player's right hip is projected out to the right slightly so that the right hip may become the centre of gravity and thereby the pivotal centre. Reaction sets in on the downswing and the player's left hip is shot out as the swing progresses to the finish.

This hip action is of the greatest importance for reasons other than its being the chief secret of the knack of keeping the player's head steady. As the illustrations show, it is the most powerful position into which you could get your body, but I will deal more fully with this point under "Dynamic laws of the golf swing". I desire to emphasize that if the hips go out in proper turn, the player's head will not sway. Study Illustration 14, and try to imagine a player projecting left hip and head to the left at the same time. It is impossible. You would lose your balance completely. You cannot project both hip and head in the same direction at the same time.

When you project your left hip to the left at the finish of the swing you naturally lean to the right to preserve your equilibrium. So too, with the right hip, at the top of the swing you will lean to the left, thereby keeping your head steady and gaining the maximum of power.

THE SHOULDER ACTION

The next important action which has a very great bearing on the steadiness of the player's head is the shoulder action. The shoulders should work in a plane perpendicular to their axis which is the upper section of the spinal column. See Illustrations 15-16-17-18-19-20.

If we did not stoop over when we played golf but stood erect, our shoulders would rotate in a perfectly horizontal course. But we do. we stoop over; the upper section of our spinal column which is the axis about which the shoulders rotate is somewhat oblique and therefore the shoulders work in an oblique course about their oblique axis.

The shoulders do not work in the same plane of obliquity as the club, but in an oblique plane of their own. The one must, however, work in perfect harmony with the other, as the slightest error on the part of the shoulders will upset the oblique plane of the club head's course.

The precise angle of obliquity in which the shoulders should work is fixed by the player's style of play, i. e., the amount of stoop assumed at the address.

9
FIRST OR ADDRESS POSITION

10
SECOND OR TOP OF
SWING POSITION
Note position of right hip,
projecting outward

11
THIRD OR FINISH OF
SWING POSITION
Player's head has and should move
forward with follow thru movement

12
HOW NOT TO SWING
A GOLF CLUB
Wrong hip action throws player's head
out of place. Note position of right hip –
drawn in. Compare with Illustration 10

13
Note position of right hip at top of swing;
projecting outward. An aphorism worth
remembering; when you swing to the
RIGHT, project your RIGHT hip out to
the RIGHT

14
Note position of left hip at finish
of swing; projecting outward.
Another important aphorism: When you
swing to the LEFT project your LEFT hip
out to the LEFT

15

16

17

18

19

20

21

A forcing exercise which quickly trains all muscles to rotate the body without moving the head. Be sure to shift your weight well from heel to heel, and form a crescent like outline down the back

22

23
Other Points To Observe To Avoid Moving The Head

1. Keep weight on heels to avoid rising on toes

2. Knees should be slightly flexed and degree of flexure not changed during the swing

3. Amount and direction of spinal bend should remain unchanged thruout swing

4. At Top and Finish of swing your feet should be within your range of vision, first over the point of the left shoulder at Top of swing, and at Finish over the right. See Illustrations 13 and 14. Were I to glance downward in the direction of my feet I would be able to see them without changing my waist bend or body position

5. Form a rough crescent-like outline down the back from back of head to left heel at Top of swing. To right heel at Finish of swing. See Illustrations 10 and 11

Part 1 – GEOMETRICS
Learn of the Five Mechanical
Laws of the Golf Swing

FUNDAMENTAL 2
Maintain a Proper
Swing Radius

LEFT ARM IS MASTER ARM

To maintain swing radius, keep left arm stiff at elbow joint. Note that I do not say straight but stiff. Just how straight or bent the arm might be is a mere matter of individual style. My point is not to change its bend. Fundamental 2 is maintenance of swing radius.

The triceps muscle keeps left arm straight. Train it to do so, become conscious of this muscle tensing. A good way to become conscious of its presence is to go to the Top of the swing, stiffen the left arm as straight as possible, ask your instructor to try to bend your arm while you resist, then with your right hand feel for the two principal heads of this muscle. The larger head will be found well under the arm close to the armpit, the other lies across the outside of the upper arm like a finger. See Illustrations 28 and 29.

Illustrations 24, 25, 26 and 27, show the rigidity of the left arm at various stages of three different swings.

LEFT ARM SHOULD ACT AS A LEVER

Of course the swing is not a true circle; it is elliptic, due to the wrist action. The wrist action, however, is not likely to spoil your radius work, while the bending of the left arm is certain to. It is also certain to cause great loss of power, since the left arm should act as a lever. A lever that breaks in the middle is no lever at all.

The golf stroke is the result of a combination of leverages – it is compound leverage. The club is one lever actuated from the left wrist. The left arm is another lever actuated from the shoulder joint. The left shoulder is another lever actuated from the spinal column. The right shoulder, right arm, and right hand operate or drive thru the club, left arm, and left shoulder levers.

Another argument in favor of keeping the left arm stiff at the elbow is that it permits a more extensive wrist action. Bend the elbow at the top of the swing and the wrist must fail to bend by just so much. Wrist action is worth more than elbow action because it is speedier.

24
Address for quarter swing
Note: Rigidity of left arm

25
Top of three-quarter swing
Note: Rigidity of left arm

26
Top of quarter swing
Note: Rigidity of left arm

27
Driving; half way down
Note: Rigidity of left arm

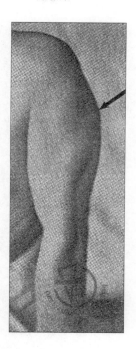

28
Triceps muscle of the left arm

29
Pupil locating the triceps muscle

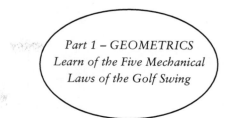

Part 1 – GEOMETRICS
Learn of the Five Mechanical
Laws of the Golf Swing

FUNDAMENTAL 3
Swing Club in a
Proper Oblique Plane

RIGHT ARM CONTROLS OBLIQUITY

The golf swing is all on a slope, i.e., it is Oblique. Right arm controls obliquity.

Club head travels in an obliquely elliptic course about the player's head.

Obliquity is determined by distance of ball from player, and the style of the player's swing, i. e., flat, orthodox or upright.

Club should travel not merely in an oblique course but in an oblique plane which must pass thru the centre of the ball. To be orthodox, hands and club head should be in the same plane with the swing centre and the ball.

The oblique plane of the swing varies greatly in the matter of style. A short player of powerful physique using longish clubs would stand further from the ball than a tall player of slender physique using shortish clubs. The degree of obliquity would be more upright for the tall player, and flat for the shorter player, and in every case if club heads, hands, swing centre and ball be all in the same plane, the swing is orthodox on this point whatever the degree of obliquity may be.

The degree of obliquity varies not only with different players, but with each individual. With the shorter clubs such as the mashie, we make a more upright swing because we stand nearer the ball; swing centre is more nearly over the ball, and therefore the plane from the ball to swing centre is more upright, and the club head, and hands should work in this same plane.

What is Known as the Flat Swing

Illustrations 32 and 33 show what is known as the flat swing: club head, hands and ball are all in the same plane tho not in a plane with the shoulder centre. This kind of swing is all right; it will produce good results, because it is mechanically correct, merely slightly unorthodox in style. Restricted vertical arm action is the cause of a flat swing. Study Illustration 30. The upward arm action has elevated hands and club heads more than the flat swing shown in Illustration 32. Had there been a little more upward action of the right arm in the swing shown in Illustration 32, the swing would not have been flat.

Right Arm Must Glide Through a Proper Slope

I emphasize the right arm because while the left arm must necessarily also rise with the right, the right arm is the controlling arm so far as the oblique plane of the swing is concerned.

Too upright a swing is frequently the cause of overswinging, i. e. swinging the club back over the shoulder beyond horizontal. When overswinging is due to this, the cure is obvious – restrict the upward action of the right arm. Overswinging is never caused by excessive backward bending of the wrists, but only by bending the left elbow or raising the hands too high. You cannot bend the wrists back too far.

The Common Cause of Topping the Ball

Illustrations 34 and 35 show a flat swing which is worthless, being both unorthodox and mechanically incorrect. The club would not connect with the ball at all. These illustrations are given to show the common cause of topping the ball with the heel of the club, which would be the result if this fault were not carried to the extremity shown. The club always follows in the plane of the arm action, indicated by the line of the shaft. Place a straight edge along the line of the shaft on Illustration 34, 35, 38, 39, 40, and 41, and it will be found that club head and hands are not in the same plane with the ball, and therefore the swing is mechanically incorrect and it would be unreasonable to expect satisfactory results. In illustrating these faults I have exaggerated them so that the student will readily see the point. Err ever so slightly in these directions and the resulting ball's flight will be unsatisfactory.

Players sometimes fall heir to a persistent malady, and for lack of understanding cannot cure it. 'Socketing' the ball with iron clubs is frequently due to too flat a swing.

THE UPRIGHT SWING

Illustrations 36 and 37 show the upright swing which tho unorthodox is mechanically correct – centre of club head, hands, and ball are all in the same plane. Note elevated position of hands relative to height of swing centre, and compare with the flat swing shown in Illustrations 32 and 33.

Unorthodoxy of swing in the matter of uprightness or flatness comes from too much or not enough vertical arm action.

30
Near TOP of mechanically correct
swing; club head, hands, centre of
shoulders, and ball all in line
orthodox style

31
Near FINISH of mechanical correct
swing; club head, hands, centre of
shoulders, and ball all in line
orthodox style

32
Near TOP of flat swing
Mechanically correct, but unorthodox
style; swing too flat

33
Near FINISH of flat swing
mechanically correct, but unorthodox
style; swing too flat

●●●

When swing is made as in illustrations 32 and 33
results should be good, because: while unorthodox in
style, mechanical essentials are correct; club head and
hands are in a plane with the ball.

34
Near top of flat swing, which is both
unorthodox and mechanically incorrect

35
Near finish of flat swing, which is
both unorthodox style, and
mechanically incorrect

•••

When swing is faulty as in illustrations 34 and 35,
result: if any, will be a topped ball off the heel of the
club Cure: make swing more upright.

36
Near top of upright swing
mechanically correct, but unorthodox
style; swing too upright

37
Near finish or upright swing
mechanically correct, but unorthodox,
swing too upright

•••

When swing is made as in illustrations 36 and 37,
results should be good because, while unorthodox in
style, mechanical essentials are correct; club head and
hands are in a plane with the ball.

38
Near top of upright swing,
which is both unorthodox style and
mechanically incorrect

39
Near finish of upright swing,
which is both unorthodox style and
mechanically incorrect

•••

When swing is faulty as in illustrations 38 and 39,
results: if any, will be off nose of club, and there will be
"Sclaffing", i. e. pounding the ground with the sole of
the club.

40
Near top of upright swing,
which is both unorthodox and
mechanically incorrect

41
Near finish of upright swing,
which is both unorthodox and
mechanically incorrect

•••

Illustrations 40 and 41 show club head in line with ball
and shoulder centre but hands are not. Violations of
plane of obliquity shown in illustrations 38, 39, 40 and
41 cause "Sclaffing", and ball if struck will be struck
with nose of club.

Part 1 – GEOMETRICS
Learn of the Five Mechanical
Laws of the Golf Swing

FUNDAMENTAL 4
Swing in parallel with line of play

SHOULDERS MUST:

A Turn to a Proper EXTENT each way

B Turn at a Proper TIME

C Turn at a Proper SPEED to guide club along the line of play

The club should swing in parallel with the line of play. Properly blended lateral motion controls the parallel of the swing. Lateral motion is created chiefly by the shoulder rotary action.

We may therefore regard the shoulder rotary action as the predominating factor in the control of the parallelism of the swing.

Side action of the arms and twisting of the wrists will also create a lateral motion, but the chief work of the arms and wrists is to create vertical motion. The shoulder rotary motion converts the arm and wrist vertical motion into a parallel swing. The shoulder rotary motion creates a round about scythe-like sweeping motion, while the arms and wrists create an up-and-down hammering-like motion.

THE PROPER BLENDING

It is the proper blending or co-ordination of the combined arm and wrist upward-and-downward movements with the shoulder-round-about movement that makes a parallel swing. To be orthodox in the full swing shoulders should turn exactly 90° each way. This leaves the arms and wrists free to make a purely upward and downward hammering motion. Thus you gain the maximum of power from all. The extent of the lateral motion each way must always be equal, to make the swing parallel. By varying the extent of the vertical motion we vary the length of our different strokes.

It is the proper extent of lateral rotation (each way right and left) done at the proper time and at the proper speed in relation to the up and down motion that makes proper blending.

Illustrations 42, 43, 44, and 45, gives a good idea of what is meant by making the swing parallel with the line of play. These pictures were taken from overhead.

SWING BEING OUT OF PARALLEL

Illustrations 46, 47, 48 and 49, show what is meant by a swing being out of parallel. This is a very common fault which causes a chronic curved flight to the right, or a misdirected flight straight out to the left of intended direction, depending on how the hands work.

Illustrations 50, 51, 52 and 53, show a swing out of parallel the other way. This causes either a misdirected flight straight out to the right of intended line of play or a curved flight to the left, known as a hook. The hook is the most likely result. The wrists in this case are apt to get the club head thru too soon for since the shoulders have turned too far to the right they are behind in their action and thus disorganize the timing of the swing.

Frequently a player might make a swing in which during the upswing and at the top of the swing all has been in perfect parallel, but on the way down the shoulders might race ahead too much and swerve the club out of the proper parallel. This brings the club into contact with the ball before the wrists have fully recovered from their sag and this combination causes a slice. The ball starts out to the left of the direct line and swerves round to the right. If the club head is not sagging behind at the point of impact, the result will be a misdirected ball starting out to the left and continuing straight on out to the left; but generally the club head will be behind because the racing ahead of the shoulders disorganizes the timing of the swing.

PARALLELISM OF SWING:
Pictures taken from overhead thru the oblique plane of the swing.

42
TOP OF SWING: Correct parallel

43
PART WAY DOWN: Correct parallel

44
PART WAY UP TO FINISH:
Correct parallel

45
FINISH OF SWING: Correct parallel

46
TOP OF SWING:
Incorrect; out of parallel

47
PART WAY DOWN:
Incorrect; out of parallel

48
PART WAY UP TO FINISH:
Incorrect; out of parallel

49
FINISH OF SWING:
Incorrect; out of parallel

•••

Incorrect Swing; Out of parallel, generally destroys the timing of the wrist snap and makes their action sluggish. This combination of errors results in a form of swing commonly known as dragging across the ball, causing a slice in which the ball starts out to left of direct line of play and curves around to right. Shoulders did not turn enough to the right at top of swing, and too much to the left at finish.

50
TOP OF SWING:
Incorrect; out of parallel

51
PART WAY DOWN:
Incorrect; out of parallel

52
PART WAY UP TO FINISH:
Incorrect; out of parallel

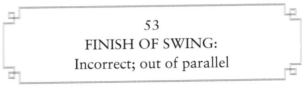

53
FINISH OF SWING:
Incorrect; out of parallel

•••

Incorrect Swing: Out of parallel, generally destroys timing of wrist snap and makes their action too vigorous to balance the shoulder effort. This combination of errors results in a form of swing commonly known as shoving across the ball, causes a hook; ball starts out to right of direct line of play and curves around to left. Shoulders turned too far to the right at top of swing, not far enough at finish.

Part 1 – GEOMETRICS
Learn of the Five Mechanical
Laws of the Golf Swing

FUNDAMENTAL 5
Strike with square impact

HANDS SHOULD CONTROL THE ANGLE OF THE CLUB FACE

During impact, club face should be at right angles to the desired direction of the ball's flight.

Hand mastery over club controls this.

Prevent both "supination", and "pronation" of club face. Correct set of the hands controls this.

"Pronation" means to turn the club face Prone, i. e., face downward.

"Supination" means just the opposite, i. e., face upward.

Correct *set* of the hands varies with the individual. Different individuals have different peculiarities of forearm development. A tendency to "slice" or "hook", might be corrected by a certain *set* of the hands.

"Slice" is only that part of the ball's flight in which the ball curves to the right. A ball driven *straight* out to the right is not sliced, but merely a misdirected flight.

"Hook" is only that part of the ball's flight in which the ball curves to the left. A ball driven *straight* out to the left is merely a misdirected flight.

THE "SET" OF THE HANDS

Illustration 54, shows the orthodox "Setting" of the two hands.

The "Set" of the hands means the extent to which they are set over or under the club handle. It will be seen in this illustration that the two angles formed by the thumb and fore part of the hand are like inverted V's with the point pointing straight upward to the player's head. Illustration 55 shows the two V's pointing to the player's right shoulder. Illustration 56 shows the two V's pointing to the player's left shoulder.

Some players, especially beginners, are very prone to allow the hands and consequently the club face to twist at the instant of impact, as shown in Illustration 55. There are two causes for this:

1. Insufficient effort on the part of the hands to control the angle at which the club should face during the impact. The resulting flight is a slice, with excessively high trajectory in which the ball starts immediately out to the right of intended direction of play. When the club faces as shown in illustration 55, it is said to have "supinated", and causes this particular class of slice.

2. Incorrect set of the hands will also cause the club face to supinate at the moment of impact.

The cure is obvious – the hands must either make greater effort to control the facing of the club at the point of impact, or be set with the V's pointing more nearly towards the right shoulder at the outset when taking the grip of the club, with club facing square to the desired direction of play. This might be the only proper setting of the hands for the particular individual concerned, and because this is perhaps the natural way for the hands to act when the muscles of the forearms are placed under the intense tension of the stroke.

MUSCLES IN THE FOREARMS

There are muscles in the forearms known as the "Supinators"; which turn the hands palm upward, and the "Pronators" which turn the hands palm downward. These muscles control the angle at which the club faces.

54
Square impact
Orthodox set of the hands

55
Supination impact
Causes excessively high trajectory,
misdirection to right and slice

56
Pronation impact
Causes smothered flight; ball starts out to
left curving to left and ducks downward

57
Collapse of left wrist
Causes immediate misdirection to right,
low trajectory and slice

●●●

Some people are very peculiarly developed in these
muscles having one of them considerably stronger than
the others, due perhaps to some peculiar occupation.
Naturally the stronger muscle exercises a greater

influence over the hands than the weaker, and therefore twists the hands and consequently the club face in its particular direction of action.

The pronators of the right arm would naturally pronate the club face, i. e. turn it prone or face downwards. This is why no hard and fast rule can be laid down as the correct set of the hands that will hold good for all players.

RIGHT FOREARM AT THE INSTANT OF IMPACT

Some players are very prone to pronate excessively with the Pronator Radii teres muscle of their right forearm at the instant of impact, which imparts a smothered, hooked flight to the ball. The ball starts out to the left and curves yet further to the left, and suddenly ducks downward, running a good distance along the ground.

There are two cures for this fault but first must be determined the real cause. The causes might be: 1 Right hand is overruling the left hand, because the left hand is allowing it to. The cure is – grip firmer with the left hand and looser with the right. 2 One or both hands may be set wrongly, the two V's being set so that they point too much towards the right shoulder, and during the stroke the hands refuse to remain so set, they twist over to the left and thereby twist the club head also. See Illustration 56.

Some players are very strongly inclined to set their hands with V's pointing towards the right shoulder, in spite of the fact that it is not the correct setting for them. The only proper cure for this, since the hands are inclined to twist over, is to set them in a position already twisted over at the outset when gripping the club, as shown in illustration 56, but of course with the club face square to the line of play. Uncomfortable as this might be, it is a certain cure for "smothering" the ball – certain because you eliminate the cause. Never combat one error with another, but eliminate the error. Suffer the discomfort till it no longer is uncomfortable. By perseverance and determination you will soon find comfort in the new habit. Console yourself with the thought that the club face must be absolutely square to the desired direction of play at and thruout the duration of impact if the ball's flight is to be true, and therefore, there is no alternative.

BALANCED EFFORT

Balanced effort on the part of the pronators and supinators of both arms is the thing to be sought, and each individual must experiment and find out exactly what particular setting of the hands produces this balanced effect. All the supinating and pronating muscles are involved in the control of the club face.

It is very important that the palm of the right hand be firmly pressed against the thumb of the left hand, then the one hand will be braced and steadied by the other.

Lock the pronators against each other in the hand setting found to be correct.

ACT AS A FULCRUM

Another cause of failure to get a square impact is shown

in Illustration 57. The left hand should act as a fulcrum against which the right hand strikes. Should this fulcrum collapse or give way, the club head will drag behind, and the club face will consequently not be square to the line of play, nor will it be perpendicular to the initial line of trajectory.

BACK PRESSURE FROM THE LEFT HAND

A common failing among players is the inability to get the club head thru; it drags behind the hands. Collapse of the left wrist is the cause. The left wrist gives way or collapses because of a lack of back pressure from the left hand against the club handle, due to its feeble effort in this direction, or due to its inability to hold its own under the strain of excessive shoulder rotary effort imposed upon it.

The cures are obvious: first determine the true cause of the trouble. Is the left hand loafing or are the shoulders overstraining? Either increase the effort of the left hand or moderate the effort of the shoulders; perhaps both are a little at fault.

Just how the left hand functions as a fulcrum is explained more fully in Transmission of power, Fundamental 12.

The resulting flight from this fault is – ball departs immediately out to the right of intended direction, flying very low with curve to the right.

SUMMARY OF THE MECHANICS OF THE GOLF SWING

MECHANICAL LAWS OF THE GOLF SWING

Meaning only those things which have to do with the order of our movements.

FIVE MECHANICAL LAWS

To strike always with the centre the the club face, observe Fundamentals 1, 2, and 3.

To strike always with club face travelling in right direction, observe Fundamental 4.

To strike always with club face at right angles to line of play, observe Fundamental 5.

These five Mechanical Laws give a working theory that is complete in so far as the order of your movements is concerned, as they cover every possible error of the swing that would cause inaccuracy of impact and thereby faulty direction. Therefore no matter what the inaccuracy might be, a perfectly clear, logical and sound reason can be found and a remedy applied. Of course there is an endless number of minor causes that upset each of these Fundamentals, but the first thing to determine always is which Fundamental was violated. It is then a comparatively easy matter to trace out the minor cause. The object of all this theory is to give you a simple and definite way of reasoning out the cause of any and all of your golf swing troubles.

These Fundamentals are the foundation of every stroke in the game no matter what the style of the player may be and they cannot be violated in the slightest degree with impunity.

FAULTS RESULTING FROM MECHANICAL ERRORS OF SWING

The common faults are: topping, skying, slicing, and hooking. These take various forms and are the result of violating the mechanical laws of the golf swing.

TOPPING

Topping is caused chiefly by the raising of the player's head, but it is quite common to top by contracting the radius of the swing, or by flattening the oblique plane of the swing. Contraction of the radius is sure to result in a top off the toe of the club, while too flat a swing will result in a top off the heel. Simply raising the player's head results in a top midway between toe and heel. When topping is the fault, determine first whether it is a top off the toe, heel, or centre. By this you will know what is the cause of the topping. When the cause is known it is a simple matter to apply a remedy.

Of course it is quite possible to cause a top off the heel by rising on the toes and losing the balance forward. However, this is going into combinations of errors, which will be dealt with later.

SKYING

The antithesis of what is said concerning topping the ball applies to skying the ball. Extension of the radius of the swing extends the club head so that it goes under the ball and this skying will be accompanied with slice, since extension of radius extends the club head outward as well as downward. Therefore the ball will be struck *inside* the centre of the club face. Too upright a swing will cause the club head to go under the ball, thereby skying it, and this skying will be accompanied with hook, to change the obliquity of the swing in this manner brings the club head in nearer to the player, and therefore the ball will be struck with the toe end of the club face.

Simply dropping the player's head, drops the centre of the club head under the ball, and the ball will be skyed without slice or hook.

The same errors that cause skying cause 'Sclaffing'.

SLICING

Slices may be divided into four different classes; each the result of a different cause.

Class 1 Slice. Definition – The ball travels two thirds of its journey quite straight on the intended line of play and only at end of its flight does it curve off to the right. This is caused by striking the ball somewhat inside the centre of the club face. To determine the cause of this fault first determine whether the height of the ball's trajectory is medium, high or low.

If class 1 slice is accompanied with medium height of flight, then Fundamental 1 is being violated, swing centre is being moved slightly forward by the player not retaining a perfect balance and the ball is being struck somewhat inside the centre of the club face.

If class 1 slice is accompanied with excessively high flight, Fundamental 2 is probably being violated – radius of the swing is being slightly extended, ball is being struck inside centre of club face, also club head is getting too much under the ball. This slice was explained under skying - the skyed slice.

If class 1 slice is accompanied with low flight, the probable cause of the trouble is violation of Fundamental 3, obliquity of swing has gone wrong. A slightly flat swing of incorrect flatness will cause impact with the lower heel corner of the club face. This always causes a low flying slice curving off at the end of the flight.

Slight violation of Fundamental 1, 2, or 3 in the manner described will cause slicing, and if carried far enough will cause socketing, or even a complete missing of the ball.

Class 2 Slice. Definition – ball starts out to the left of the direct line of play and immediately begins to swerve to the right. This is because the club face strikes the ball a glancing blow, dragging across the line of play from outside line of play to inside. The cause is that the swing is out of parallel with the line of play. Fundamental 4 is being violated. See Illustrations 46, 47, 48, and 49. Also the wrists are snapping too late.

Class 3 Slice. Definition – ball starts immediately to the right, flying excessively high. Supination of the club face is the trouble. Fundamental 5 is being violated. See Illustration 55.

Class 4 Slice. Definition – ball starts immediately to the right flying low. Left wrist as a fulcrum is giving way, another form of violation of Fundamental 5. See Illustration 57.

It is quite possible to have a combination of several slicing causes at work.

HOOKING

The opposite of what is said of slicing applies to hooking. There are four distinct classes of hooks, the class 1, having sub-classifications the same as the slice.

Class 1 Hook. Definition – the ball travels two thirds of its journey quite straight on the intended line of play and only at the end of its flight does it curve off to the left. This is caused by striking the ball somewhat outside the centre of the club face. To determine the cause of this fault, first determine whether the ball's trajectory is high, medium or low. If low then the probable error is violation of Fundamental 2 – radius is being slightly contracted.

If class 1 hook is accompanied with high flight, the probable cause of the trouble is violation of Fundamental 3, obliquity of swing has gone wrong. A slightly upright swing of incorrect uprightness will cause impact with the upper toe corner of the club face. This always causes a high flying hook curving off at the end of the flight.

Class 1 hook with normal trajectory is due to violation of Fundamental 1; swing centre is being moved slightly backward by the player not retaining a perfect balance. The minor matter, i.e., the cause of loss of balance, is a thing which can be determined only by close observation. It might be caused by the player's standing too far away from the ball with the body-weight upon the balls of the feet and settling back upon the heels during the swing. The cure in a case of this kind would be to stand nearer the ball, with the body weight on the heels. This is the proper place to have it for every stroke.

Class 2 Hook. Definition – ball starts out to the right of the direct line of play and immediately begins to swerve to the left. This is because the club face strikes the ball a glancing blow, cutting across the line of play from inside the line of play to outside. The trouble is that the swing is out of parallel. Fundamental 4 is being violated. See Illustrations 50, 51, 52, and 53. Also the wrists are snapping too soon.

Class 3 Hook. Definition – ball starts immediately to the left and curving yet further to the left suddenly ducks downward and runs a good distance along the ground. Pronation of the club face is the trouble. Fundamental 5 is being violated, right hand is overruling the left.

Class 4 Hook. Definition – ball starts immediately to the left, flying high. Left hand as a fulcrum is not giving way but is offering too great a resistance to the right hand and is therefore getting the club head thru too soon. This is another form of violation of Fundamental 5. The effort of the hands is unbalanced or badly timed.

MISDIRECTION
Misdirection is caused by faulty hand control of the angle at which the club faces during impact, and also by the swing being out of parallel due to faulty rotary shoulder action. Violation of Fundamental 4, 5.

SIMPLE SUMMARY OF SWING CONTROL

THE FIVE FUNDAMENTALS

To put the essence of all the foregoing on Mechanics into simple language, the five Fundamentals are:

1. HEAD: Keep it steady, to keep the whole swing steady.

2. LEFT ARM: Keep it stiff, to preserve the swing radius.

3. RIGHT ARM: With it raise the club to a proper height to guide it thru a proper slope.

4. SHOULDERS: Turn them the proper amount each way, and at the proper time, and at the proper speed to guide the club along the line of play.

5. HANDS: Work with them to the utmost of their strength at the moment of impact, to control the club face so that it will be square to desired direction of play.

If you are not hitting your ball true and sending it straight, one or more of these five Fundamentals have gone wrong. Find out which and correct it.

OLD TOM TELLING
HIS STORY

*AN EXTRACT FROM "GOLF" BY HORACE G.
HUTCHINSON WITH CONTRIBUTIONS BY LORD
WELLWOOD, SIR WALTER SIMPSON, BART., RIGHT
HON. A. J. BALFOUR, M.P. ANDREW LANG, H. S.
C. EVERARD, AND OTHERS WITH NUMEROUS
ILLUSTRATIONS BY THOMAS HODGE AND HARRY
FURNISS Second Edition LONDON LONGMANS,
GREEN, AND CO. 1890.*

On The Links Of Musselburgh

'Yet nearer to the smoke of Auld Reekie, on the links of
Musselburgh, we may see the game received with scarcely
less interest by the great mass of the populace. That was
a great occasion there when Bob Fergusson had to do
each of the last three holes in three a-piece to tie for the
championship-and did it! It was growing quite dusk, and
from one side to the other the course was lined with a
dense mass of spectators, gentlemen of learning, and top-

hatted, from Edinburgh, the modern Athens, shoulder to shoulder with grimy miners, who had climbed from the bowels of the earth to see them play.

The Heroes of their Time

And it is a good links, too, although so narrow, calling out all the best qualities of the golfer. A links, too, which is sanctified by the memory of many a fine match of old days, when Allan Robertson, and the Parks and Dunns of a previous generation, and old Tom Morris were the heroes of their time. It is there that, besides many other noteworthy clubs, the Honourable Company of Edinburgh Golfers have their clubhouse, and play their 'dinner matches' – matches to which zest is added by stakes large enough to promote interest, yet not large enough to cause ill feeling, wagered over their wine at their dinners in Edinburgh. And it is a links which is a fine test of golfing prowess – though there be but nine holes.

Yet the first three call for long strong driving, following, roughly, the course of the road, which forms the hazard upon the one side, while on the other are bunkers and whins which, alas! are fast going the way of all whins, so that they need the driving to be sure and straight, as well as far. Then, when we have reached 'Mrs. Forman's,' the third hole, with perhaps a visit to 'Lord Shand's bunker' by the way, we turn to our left, seawards, and leaving the clayey ground of the nature of the first five holes at St. Andrews, we come up along truer links turf, close beside – too close occasionally, if we heel our ball – the sea.

THE BROTHERS WILLIAM AND JAMES DUNN

As will have been already seen in our account of their matches against Allan Robertson and Tom Morris, the brothers William and James Dunn were in the first rank of players, and on their native green of Musselburgh were well-nigh invincible.

They were twins, club and ball makers by trade, and remained a long time at home, but subsequently removed to Blackheath. Willie Dunn in particular was distinguished for a beautiful, easy style, standing straight up to his ball, and was, as we have remarked above, an exceedingly long driver.

'Dunny'

In support of this statement, it may be said that he once played a shot from the medal tee on the Hole O' Cross Green at St. Andrews, coming in to the fourth hole, and the ball was found in the little crescent-shaped bunker at the end of the Elysian Fields; this hazard in commemoration of the shot was christened 'Dunny,' a name which it retains to this day. The distance, as measured on the map, is 250 yards, and although by no means standing as a record for length (indeed the writer has frequently seen longer shots driven), yet it will probably be admitted that anyone who could make such a shot (and in this instance the circumstances of wind and condition of ground were not exceptionally favourable) must be credited with driving powers above the average.

Dunn was tutored by Tom Morris

After he had been at Blackheath some years, a match was arranged between him and Willie Park, to be played at Prestwick. Dunn was tutored by Tom Morris, who put him through his facings every day for a week; James Dunn was also a very fine player, though not so long a driver by ten or fifteen yards as his brother; consequently it fell to the latter to uphold the family honour in single matches of importance, whilst the former took his share in foursome play, and could be relied upon as a steady, trustworthy colleague. He died unmarried; but his brother was married and left a family, one of whom is the popular and highly efficient Tom Dunn, the well-known custodian of North Berwick, formerly green-keeper at Wimbledon. He and his brother Willie maintain the family honour, both being fine players.

OLD TOM TELLING HIS STORY

The Twa Dunns, Willie and Jamie, Graund Players Baith, Nane Better

This transcript of a conversation held on New Year's Day, 1886, is not only interesting in itself, but contains much sound golfing philosophy.

I give it to the reader precisely in the shape in which it has been given to me:

'A gude new year t'ye, Maister Alexander, an' mony 0' them! An' it's come weel in, the year has; for it's just a braw day for a mautch. Lod, sir, it aye seems to me the years, as they rise, skelp fester the tane after t'ither; they'll sune be makin' auld men o've a'. Hoo auld am I, d'ye ask, sir? Weel I was born June 16, 1821; and ye can calc' late that for yoursel'. Aye! as ye say, sir, born and bred in St. Awndrews, an' a gowffer a' ma days. The vera first time, I think, I hae mind 0' mysel' I was toddlin' aboot at the short holes, wi' a putter uneath ma bit oxter.

'I was made 'prentice to Allan as a ba'-macker at eighteen, and wrocht wi' him eliven years. We played, Allan and me thegither, some geyan big mautches-ane in parteecler wi' the twa Dunns, Willie and Jamie, graund players baith, nane better -

William and James Dunn were in the first rank of players,
and on their native green of Musselburgh were well-nigh invincible.

OLD TOM

Never but on one occasion at North Berwick was old
Tom much better than a drag upon his son, and it is the
literal truth to say that at that time he did not play a
game within a third to half one of his subsequent usual
form from sixty years old till now. After passing that age
he took a new lease of play, and won two professional
competitions-one at Wemyss, the other at Hoylake;
and on his sixty-fourth birthday, June 17, 1885, he
accomplished the remarkable feat of holing St. Andrews
Links in the grand score of 81, whilst playing with Mr.
Charles Hutchings, his figures being, out 555554434;
home, 444555554. It will be observed that not a figure
above a five occurs, and what is the more extraordinary,
he had until that day never succeeded in going round
without a six somewhere in his score.

His driving is to the full as long as it ever was in
his life, and when he gets what he calls' ane of ma very

best,' the longest drivers of the present day would have their work cut out to gain any very material advantage over him. For this wonderful game he is able to play when close upon seventy years old, he has no doubt to thank the strictly temperate life he has always led; and it would be well indeed if some of the younger generation of professionals had the strength of mind to follow his example in this respect.

While Dunn took a Snuff and Smiled Satisfactorily

Space forbids any copious account of the many interesting matches he has played during his long career; his tussles with Park are the chief ones to be noticed, but he has encountered at one time or another almost every golfer of note. In a match with Willie Dunn in May 1851, the latter being dormy one, the finish is thus described: 'The last hole was in a very peculiar place at the top of a hill and Tom's ball rolled first down the east side, and the next putt sent it over again on the west. Seeing that he could not halve the match, Tom gave his ball a kick in disgust, while Dunn took a snuff, and smiled satisfactorily, having the credit of taking the match by two holes.'

SEYMOUR DUNN

An Extract From THANKS FOR THE GAME The Best of Golf with HENRY COTTON Sidgwick & Jackson London Henry Cotton Penina 1980.

"After over fifty years in the game, as a professional,

championship winner and teacher, I feel I have earned the right to speak my mind on the game of golf, hoping that my words will reach at least some of the twenty million or so people throughout the world who enjoy, and sometimes suffer from, their involvement in this greatest of all sports."

"Sixty years ago I remember that outstanding instructor Seymour Dunn proclaiming that golf was 85 per cent hands and only 15 per cent body. Nothing in a lifetime's experience in golf has happened to make me think otherwise. How right he has been!"

"Many of the old champions stressed that 'when your legs go, you are through winning'; Sam Snead during his 1979 trip to Australia announced that he was almost through with competing in the 'big leagues' for his legs had gone, and of course strong legs are essential for control. Accept this as a fact, learn to use the hands properly, and like me you will enjoy a lifetime of pleasure-golf."

Also see our web site at:
www.originalgolffundamentalsdunns5lessons.com

21530484R00059

Printed in Great Britain
by Amazon